ALL ABOUT CHRISTMAS TREES

KRISTEN RAJCZAK NELSON

PowerKiDS press.

NEW YORK

Published in 2020 by The Rosen Publishing Group, Inc.
29 East 21st Street, New York, NY 10010

First Edition

Editor: Kristen Nelson
Book Design: Reann Nye

Photo Credits: Cover Stewart Cohen/Getty Images; p. 5 YanLev/Shutterstock.com; p. 7 Leena Robinson/Shutterstock.com; p. 9 AlexMaster/Shutterstock.com; p.11 Alena Ozerova/Shutterstock.com; p. 13 MarinaDa/Shutterstock.com; p. 15 https://commons.wikimedia.org/wiki/File:Christmas_Tree_1848.jpg; p. 17 Evans/Hulton Archive/Getty Images; p. 19 Alexander Tolstykh/Shutterstock.com; p. 21 Ryan McVay/ Photodisc/Getty Images; p. 22 Andrew F. Kazmierski/Shutterstock.com.

Cataloging-in-Publication Data

Names: Rajczak Nelson, Kristen.
Title: All about Christmas trees / Kristen Rajczak Nelson.
Description: New York : PowerKids Press, 2020. | Series: It's Christmas! | Includes glossary and index.
Identifiers: ISBN 9781725300729 (pbk.) | ISBN 9781725300743 (library bound) | ISBN 9781725300736 (6pack)
Subjects: LCSH: Christmas trees–Juvenile literature.
Classification: LCC GT4989.R35 2020 | DDC 394.2663–dc23

CPSIA Compliance Information: Batch #CSPK19. For Further Information contact Rosen Publishing, New York, New York at 1-800-237-9932.

CONTENTS

WORLDWIDE CUSTOM

In countries around the world, people **celebrate** Christmas by putting up an evergreen tree. They may put **ornaments** or strings of popcorn on its branches. Some people like to put lights around it! Many families put their Christmas presents under it. But why? Where did this **custom** come from?

5

ANCIENT TIMES

Evergreen trees are those that stay green all year long. They don't lose their leaves in fall like maple or oak trees. Many **ancient** peoples, including the Chinese, Hebrews, and Egyptians, saw evergreens as **symbols** of life. Some made wreaths, or rings, out of their branches just like we do today.

In ancient northern Europe, people had winter holidays celebrating the passing of the shortest day of the year. This day is often December 21. People **decorated** with evergreens to keep evil away from their homes. The evergreens were also a reminder that spring and all things green would be coming again soon.

Likely in the fourth century, December 25 was chosen as the day to celebrate Christmas, one of the major holidays of Christianity. As the faith spread over time, Christmas celebrations and the winter holiday customs of ancient groups mixed. Soon, evergreen branches and trees had become part of Christmastime.

XMAS

FROM GERMANY AND BEYOND

The first true Christmas trees are often traced to Germany during the **Middle Ages**. There, people put up a tree on December 24 to remember a Bible story of the first people, Adam and Eve. They also put up a decorated wooden **pyramid**. These two customs came together as today's Christmas trees!

13

The idea of Christmas trees came to North America with German **colonists** settling in Pennsylvania in the 1600s. The trees' popularity grew during the 1800s because of Prince Albert of England, who was from Germany. He and Queen Victoria were known to put up a Christmas tree, spreading the custom around England and the United States.

By the 1800s, Christmas trees were also common in Switzerland, Poland, and the Netherlands. When Christian **missionaries** began traveling to Asia, they brought Christmas customs with them. People in China and Japan had Christmas trees by the 1900s! People in these countries put beautiful paper decorations on the trees.

DECORATIONS TO BUY

Christmas trees were so popular that people began making and selling ornaments in stores by the late 1800s. These ornaments were made of glass, cotton, beads, and paper. Soon, the first Christmas lights went on sale, too. The present-day look of a decorated Christmas tree was truly coming to be.

REAL, FAKE, OR FAMOUS?

Today, Christmas trees are grown in all 50 states—including Hawaii! But many people around the world don't have a real tree in their living room. Businesses began selling artificial, or fake, trees in the 1930s. Over the years, fake trees have been green, blue, silver, and even pink!

From the White House to Rockefeller Center in New York City, Christmas trees are found everywhere in the month of December. Many towns host Christmas tree lightings and families often spend an evening together choosing and decorating their tree. It's one of the most special symbols of Christmas!

ROCKEFELLER CENTER

GLOSSARY

ancient: Coming from a time that was long ago in the past.

celebrate: To mark a special day.

colonist: A person who lives in a colony, or land owned by another country.

custom: An action or way of behaving that is common among the people in a certain group or place.

decorate: To make something look nice by adding something to it.

Middle Ages: A time in Europe from about AD 500 to 1500.

missionary: Someone who travels to a place to spread their faith.

ornament: A small fancy object put on something else to make it look nice.

pyramid: A shape that is wide at the bottom and becomes narrower as it reaches the top.

symbol: Something that stands for something else.

INDEX

WEBSITES

Due to the changing nature of Internet links, PowerKids Press has developed an online list of websites related to the subject of this book. This site is updated regularly. Please use this link to access the list: www.powerkidslinks.com/IC/trees